For Lucy and Emily

J.A.

For Amelia

A.B.

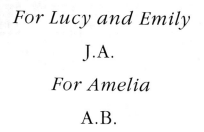

Text copyright © 1993 by Judy Allen
Illustrations copyright © 1993 by Alan Baron

First U.S. edition 1993
Published in Great Britain in 1993
by Walker Books Ltd., London.

Library of Congress Catalog Card Number 92-54623
Library of Congress Cataloging-in-Publication Data is available.

ISBN 1-56402-218-8

10 9 8 7 6 5 4 3 2 1

Printed in Hong Kong

The pictures in this book were done in pencil and watercolor.

Candlewick Press
2067 Massachusetts Avenue
Cambridge, Massachusetts 02140

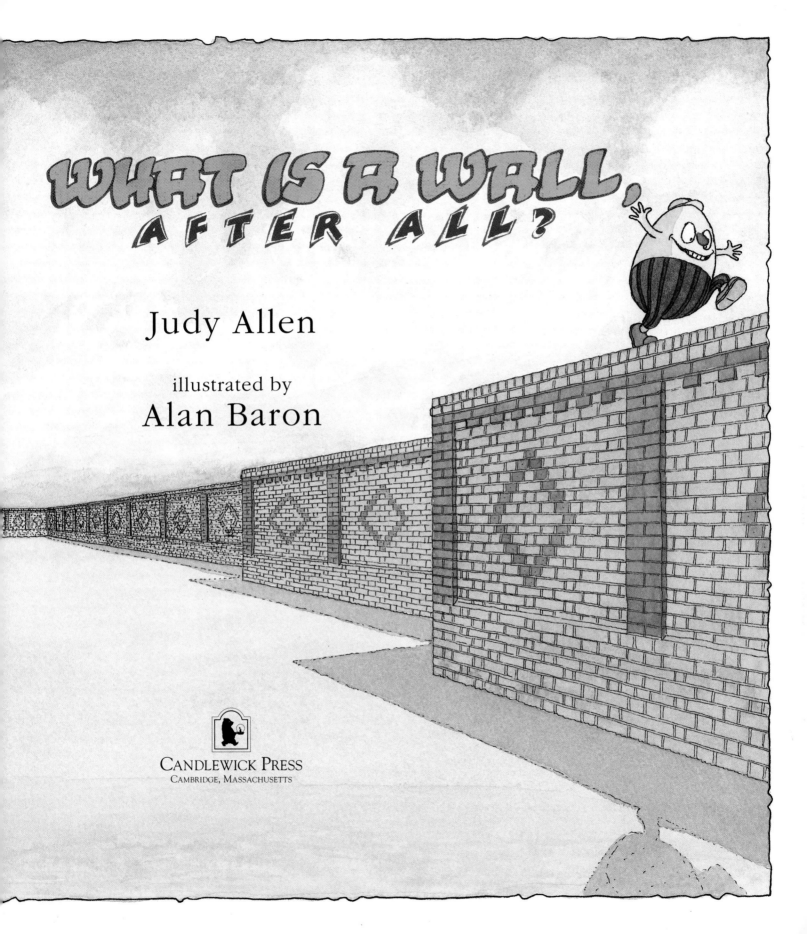

WHAT IS A WALL,
AFTER ALL?

Judy Allen

illustrated by
Alan Baron

CANDLEWICK PRESS
CAMBRIDGE, MASSACHUSETTS

Wherever you are when you open this book,

I bet you can see a wall, if you look.

Could you
build a wall?

No problem
at all!

Put brick
on brick.

Mortar makes
it stick.

It's a weak wall, a sick wall, a leaning-on-a-stick wall,
a feeble wall, a quaky wall, a crumbly, tumbly, shaky wall.

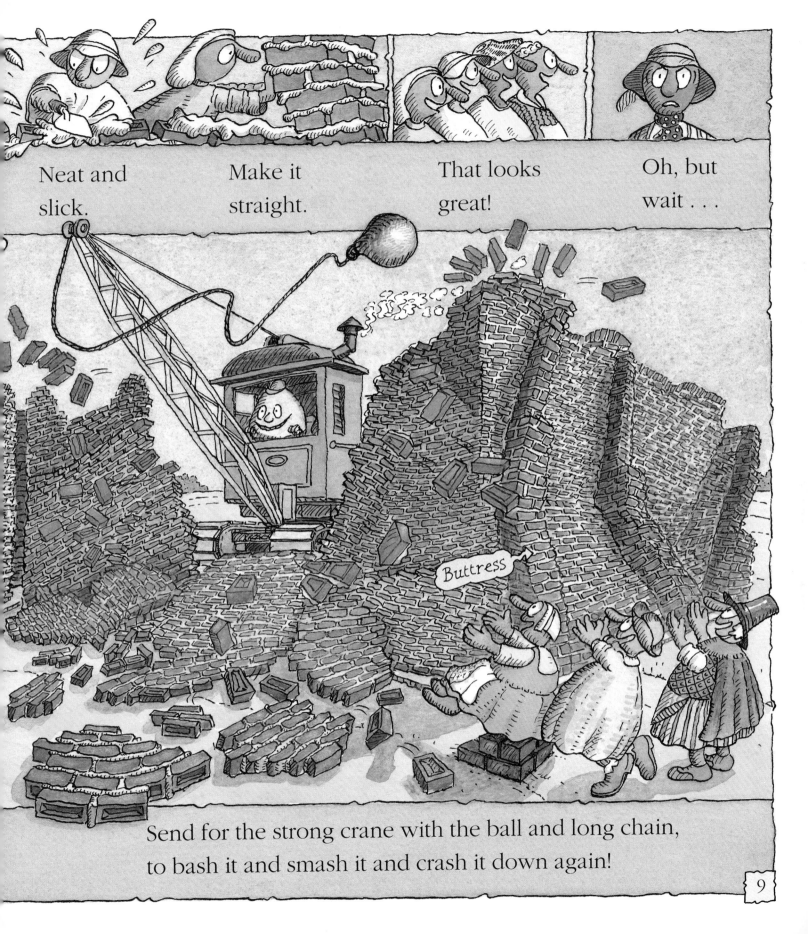

Neat and slick.

Make it straight.

That looks great!

Oh, but wait . . .

Send for the strong crane with the ball and long chain, to bash it and smash it and crash it down again!

A dry-stone wall may look like a huddle
of jagged stones, ragged stones, all in a muddle,
a jumble that could easily tumble and fall.
Look carefully, though, it's cleverly done:
Each stone is balanced on another one.
Each shape has been picked to fit its own space,
so the wall stands firm on a solid base.

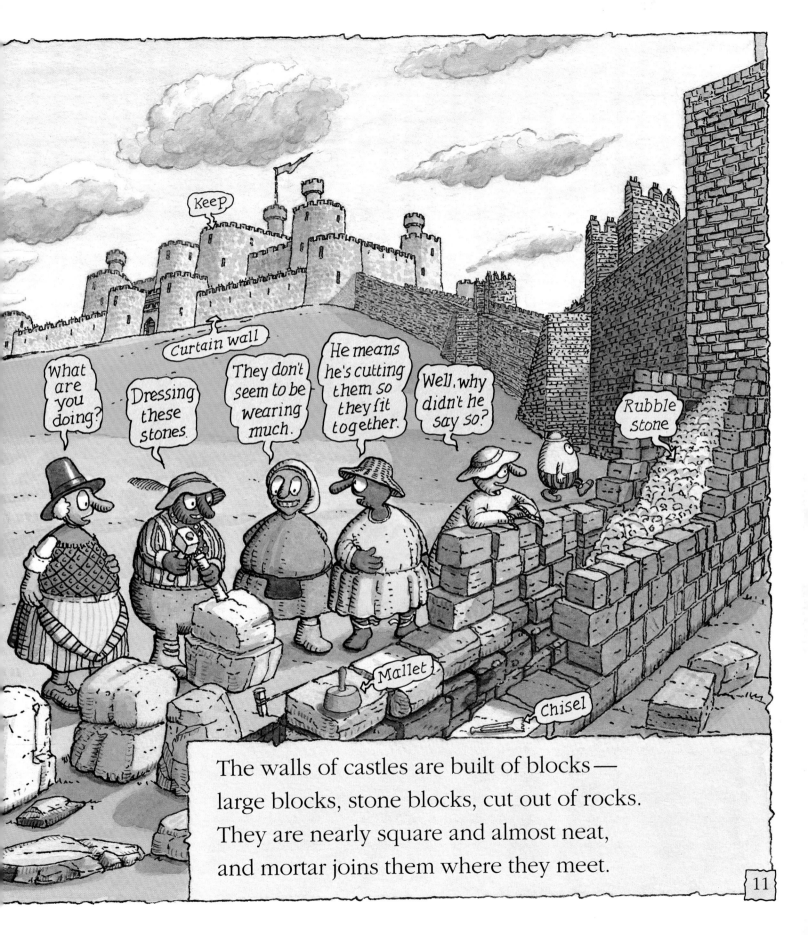

The walls of castles are built of blocks—
large blocks, stone blocks, cut out of rocks.
They are nearly square and almost neat,
and mortar joins them where they meet.

11

There are walls made of glass that shine in the sun,
and rubbery walls that are silly—but fun!

There are brick walls and thick walls and walls owned by cats,
and deep underground there are cave walls, with bats.

13

There

are

tall

walls,

high

walls,

climb

up

to

the

sky

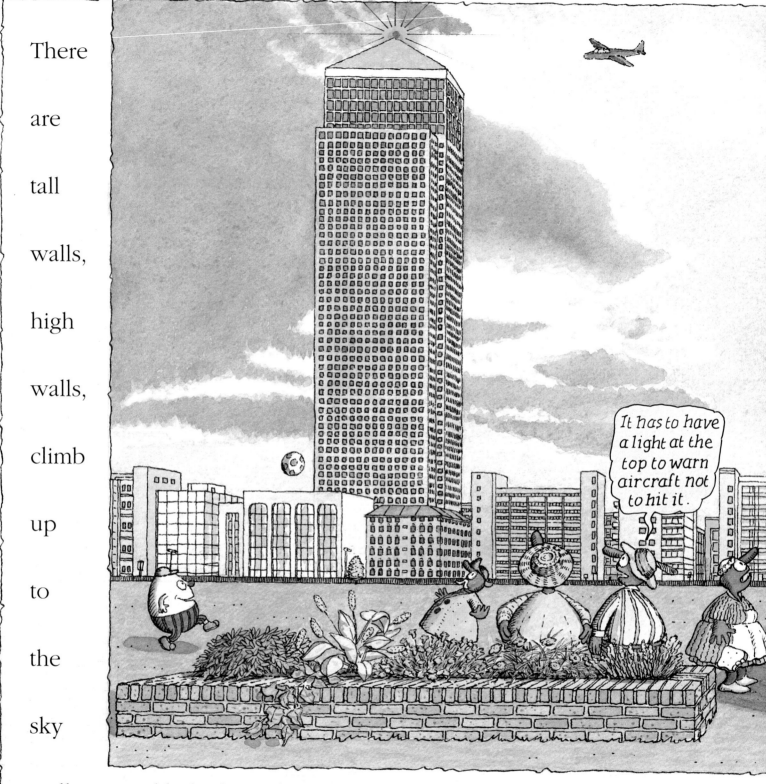

walls . . . and little, low, short walls that creep along the ground.

There are big, long, wide walls, we've-got-something-to-hide walls, and the walls of a lighthouse that have to be round.

There are walls that are horribly fierce,

There are walls that are meant to get hot,

and walls that are terribly old.

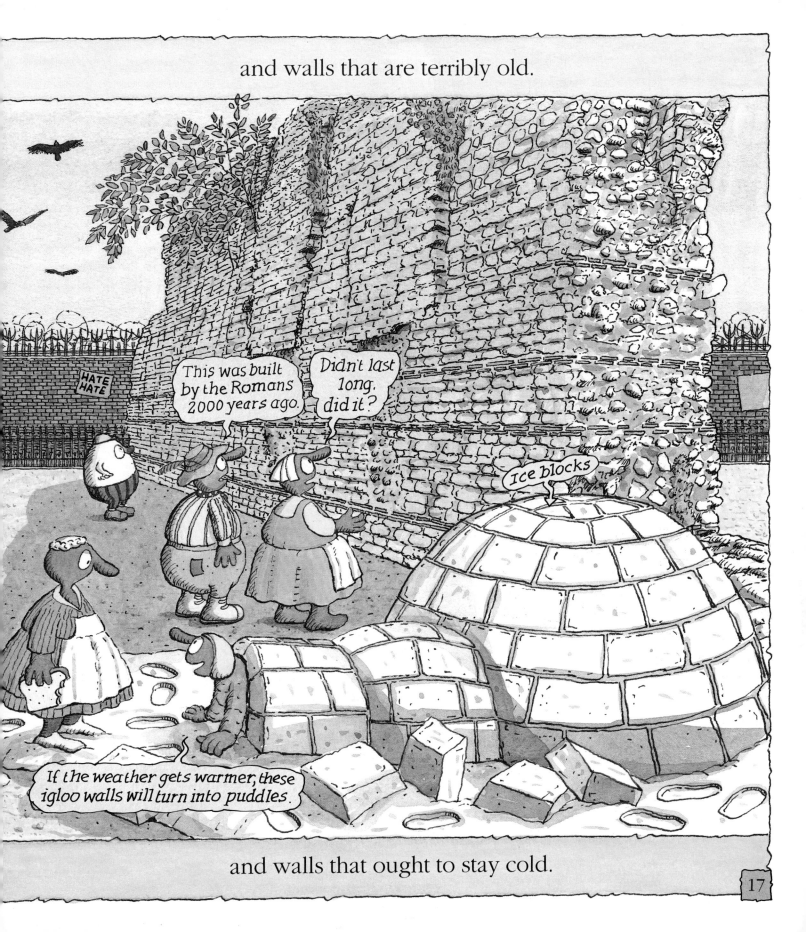

and walls that ought to stay cold.

Some walls are there to shut out invaders
(a safe keeps out robbers, a fort keeps out raiders).

18

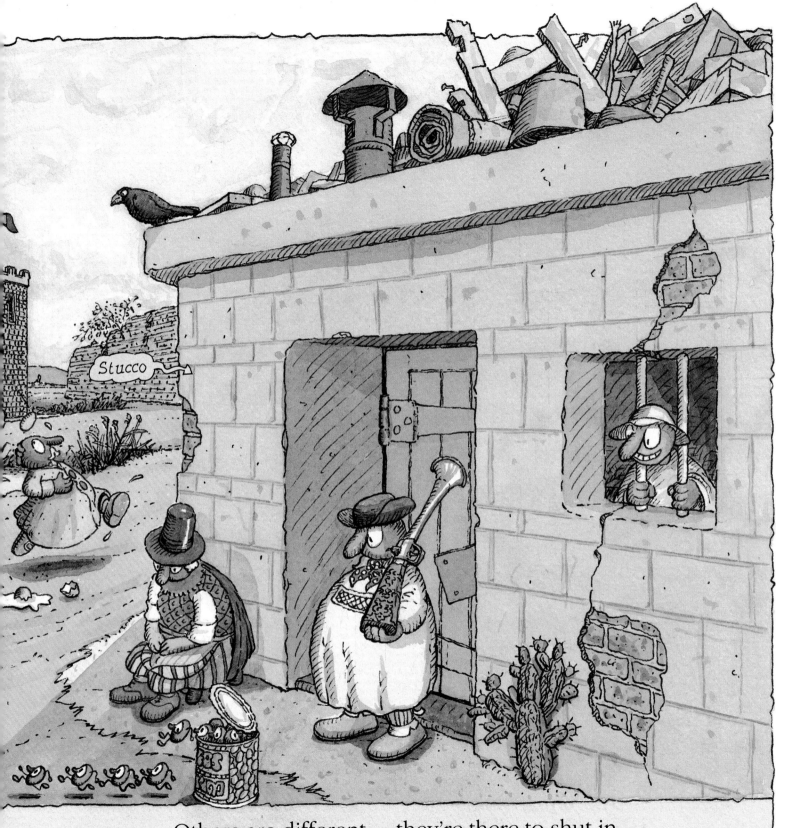

Others are different—they're there to shut in.
(Think of people in prison, or beans in a tin!)

Here is a wall that has to be tough
so it won't collapse when the weather gets rough

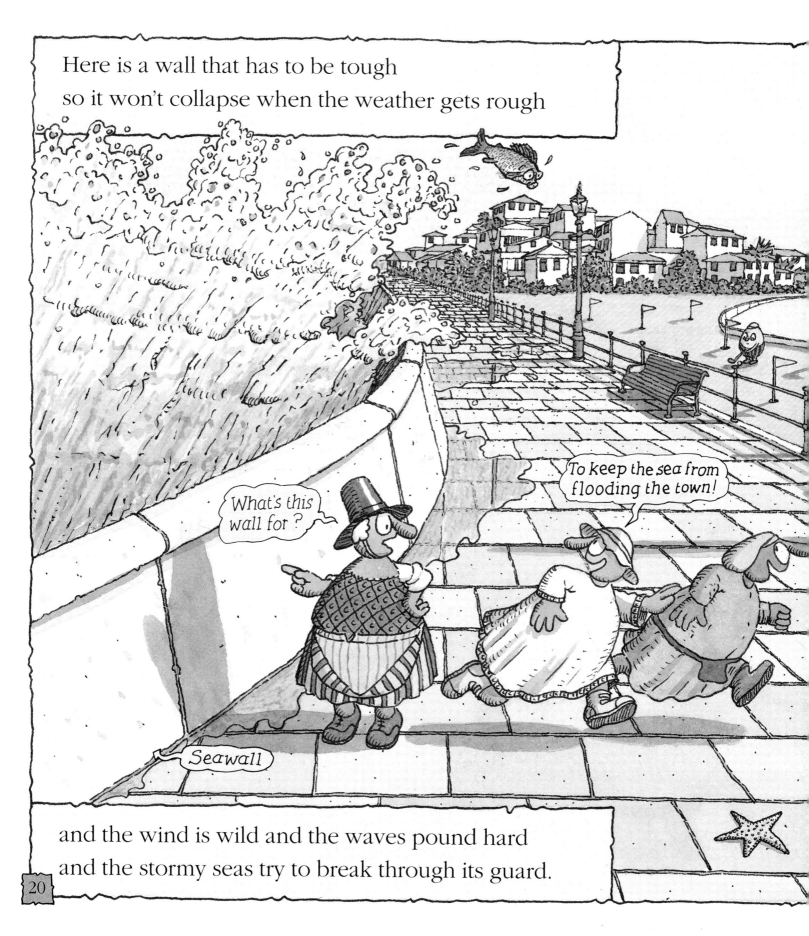

and the wind is wild and the waves pound hard
and the stormy seas try to break through its guard.

Here is a wall that is long, strong, and round:
It's the wall of a tunnel that runs underground.

The wall of this dam has to stand like a rock
to hold back the river whose path it must block.

Most indoor walls are plain and flat,

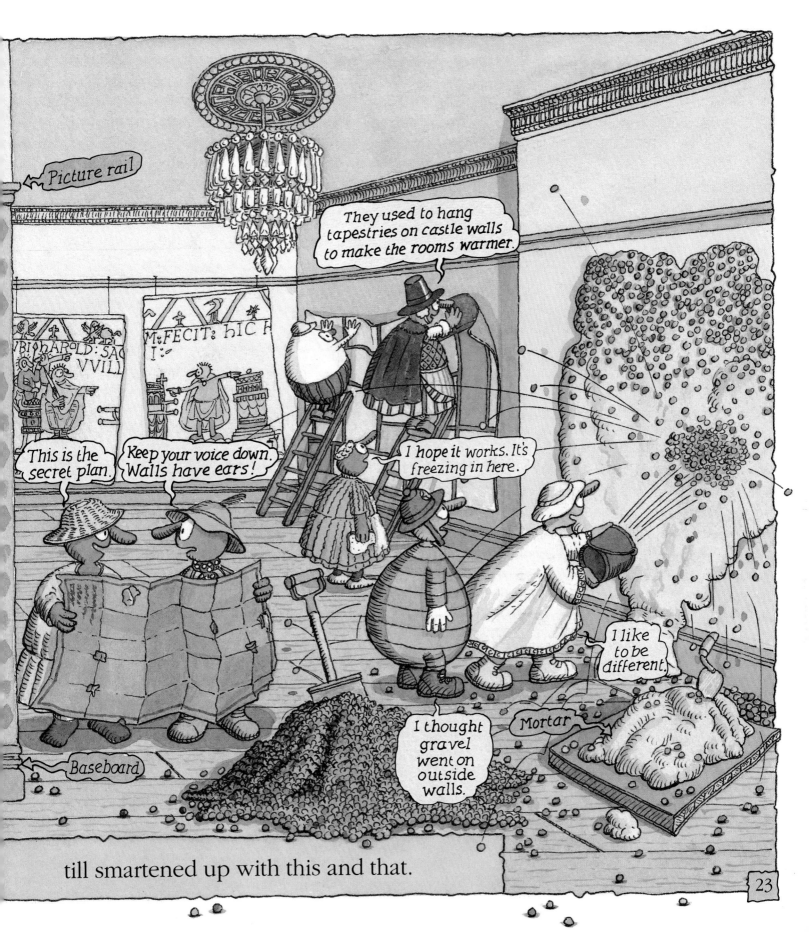

till smartened up with this and that.

23

If you sit on a wall you may not be alone.

Small things could be living in cracks in the stone.

If you want to climb a mountain wall you will probably need stout boots and crampons and pitons to hammer into narrow cracks and wedges to hammer into wide cracks and a climbing hammer to put them in with and an ice ax and a hammer ax (which is a short ice ax) and a strong rope and a helmet and warm clothes in case you freeze.

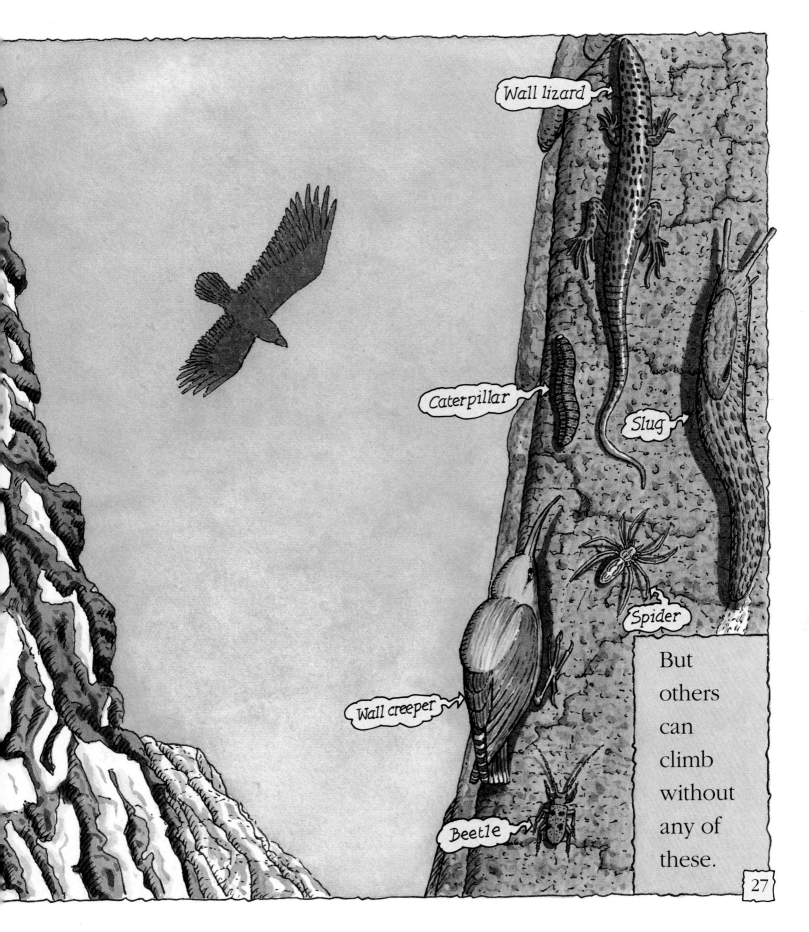

But
others
can
climb
without
any of
these.

Where are you? In a room? In a garden? In a car? A bus? A train?

In a field? On a boat? Maybe up in a plane?

In the street? On the beach? In a hot-air balloon?

In a café? In bed? Perhaps on the moon?

Well, wherever you are when you finish this book,

I bet you can see a wall, if you look.